SCHOLASTIC

READ & RESPOND

Bringing the best books to life in the classroom

Activities based on

The Lighthouse Keeper's Lunch

By Ronda and David Armitage

Terms and conditions

IMPORTANT – PERMITTED USE AND WARNINGS – READ CAREFULLY BEFORE USING

IF YOU ACCEPT THE ABOVE CONDITIONS YOU MAY PROCEED TO USE THE CD-ROM.

Recommended system requirements:
Windows: XP (Service Pack 3), Vista (Service Pack 2), Windows 7 or Windows 8 with 2.33GHz processor
Mac: OS 10.6 to 10.8 with Intel Core™ Duo processor
1GB RAM (recommended)
1024 x 768 Screen resolution
CD-ROM drive (24x speed recommended)
Adobe Reader (version 9 recommended for Mac users)
Broadband internet connections (for installation and updates)

For all technical support queries (including no CD drive), please phone Scholastic Customer Services on 0845 6039091.

Designed using Adobe Indesign
Published by Scholastic Ltd,
Book End, Range Road, Witney,
Oxfordshire OX29 0YD
www.scholastic.co.uk

Printed and bound by Ashford Colour Press
© 2015 Scholastic Ltd
1 2 3 4 5 6 7 8 9   5 6 7 8 9 0 1 2 3 4

British Library Cataloguing-in-Publication Data A catalogue record for this book is available from the British Library.
ISBN 978 1407 14220 3

Due to the nature of the web, we cannot guarantee the content or links of any site mentioned. We strongly recommend that teachers check websites before using them in the classroom.

Author Sarah Snashall
Editorial team Rachel Morgan, Jenny Wilcox, Vicky Butt, Kate Pedlar
Series designer Neil Salt
Design team Ian Foulis and Mike Connor
Illustrator Gemma Hastilow
Digital development Hannah Barnett, Phil Crothers and MWA Technologies Private Ltd

Acknowledgements
The publishers gratefully acknowledge permission to reproduce the following copyright material:

Scholastic Children's Books for the use of the cover, text and illustrations from *The Lighthouse Keeper's Lunch* by Ronda Armitage, illustrated by David Armitage. Text © 1977, Ronda Armitage. Illustration © 1977, David Armitage (2014, Scholastic Children's Books).

Every effort has been made to trace copyright holders for the works reproduced in this book, and the publishers apologise for any inadvertent omissions.

CONTENTS

▼ INTRODUCTION

Read & Respond provides teaching ideas related to a specific children's book. The series focuses on best-loved books and brings you ways to use them to engage your class and enthuse them about reading.

The book is divided into different sections:

- **About the book and author:** gives you some background information about the book and the author.

- **Guided reading:** breaks the book down into sections and gives notes for using it with guided reading groups. A bookmark has been provided on page 10 containing comprehension questions. The children can be directed to refer to these as they read.

- **Shared reading:** provides extracts from the children's books with associated notes for focused work. There is also one non-fiction extract that relates to the children's book.

- **Phonics & spelling:** provides phonics and spelling work related to the children's book so you can teach these skills in context.

- **Plot, character & setting:** contains activity ideas focussed on the plot, characters and the setting of the story.

- **Talk about it:** has speaking and listening activities related to the children's book. These activities may be based directly on the children's book or be broadly based on the themes and concepts of the story.

- **Get writing:** provides writing activities related to the children's book. These activities may be based directly on the children's book or be broadly based on the themes and concepts of the story.

- **Assessment:** contains short activities that will help you assess whether the children have understood concepts and curriculum objectives. They are designed to be informal activities to feed into your planning.

The activities follow the same format:

- **Objective:** the objective for the lesson. It will be based upon a curriculum objective, but will often be more specific to the focus being covered.

- **What you need:** a list of resources you need to teach the lesson, including digital resources (printable pages, interactive activities and media resources, see page 5).

- **What to do:** the activity notes.

- **Differentiation:** this is provided where specific and useful differentiation advice can be given to support and/or extend the learning in the activity. Differentiation by providing additional adult support has not been included as this will be at a teacher's discretion based upon specific children's needs and ability, as well as the availability of support.

The activities are numbered for reference within each section and should move through the text sequentially – so you can use the lesson while you are reading the book. Once you have read the book, most of the activities can be used in any order you wish.

Below are brief guidance notes for using the CD-ROM. For more detailed information, please click on the '?' button in the top right-hand corner of the screen.

The program contains the following:

- The extract pages from the book.
- All of the photocopiable pages from the book.
- Additional printable pages.
- Interactive on-screen activities.
- Media resources.

Getting started

Put the CD-ROM into your CD-ROM drive. If you do not have a CD-ROM drive, phone Scholastic Customer Services on 0845 6039091.

- For Windows users, the install wizard should autorun, if it fails to do so then navigate to your CD-ROM drive. Then follow the installation process.
- For Mac users, copy the disk image file to your hard drive. After it has finished copying double click it to mount the disk image. Navigate to the mounted disk image and run the installer. After installation the disk image can be unmounted and the DMG can be deleted from the hard drive.
- To install on a network, see the ReadMe file located on the CD-ROM (navigate to your drive).

To complete the installation of the program you need to open the program and click 'Update' in the pop-up. Please note – this CD-ROM is web-enabled and the content will be downloaded from the internet to your hard-drive to populate the CD-ROM with the relevant resources. This only needs to be done on first use, after this you will be able to use the CD-ROM without an internet connection. If at any point any content is updated, you will receive another pop-up upon start up when there is an internet connection.

Main menu

The main menu is the first screen that appears. Here you can access: terms and conditions, registration links, how to use the CD-ROM and credits. To access a specific book click on the relevant button (NB only titles installed will be available). You can filter by the

drop-down lists if you wish. You can search all resources by clicking 'Search' in the bottom left-hand corner. You can also login and access favourites that you have bookmarked.

Resources

By clicking on a book on the Main menu, you are taken to the resources for that title. The resources are divided into categories: Media, Interactives, Extracts and Printables. Select the category and then launch a resource by clicking the play button.

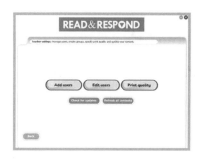

Teacher settings

In the top right-hand corner of the screen is a small 'T' icon. This is the teacher settings area. It is password protected, the password is: login. This area will allow you to choose the print quality settings for interactive activities ('Default' or 'Best') and also allow you to check for updates to the program or re-download all content to the disk via Refresh all content. You can also set up user logins so that you can save and access favourites. Once a user is set up, they can enter by clicking the login link underneath the 'T' and '?' buttons.

Search

You can access an all resources search by clicking the search button on the bottom-left of the Main menu.

You can search for activities by type (using the drop-down filter) or by keyword by typing into the box. You can then assign resources to your favourites area or launch them directly from the search area.

CURRICULUM LINKS

Section	Activity	Curriculum objectives
Guided reading		Comprehension: To discuss the significance of the title and events.
		Comprehension: To participate in discussion about books.
Shared reading	1	Word reading: To respond speedily with the correct sound to graphemes. (Covers long /igh/.)
		Comprehension: To discuss word meanings.
	2	Comprehension: To discuss word meaning and the sequence of events.
	3	Comprehension: To be introduced to non-fiction books that are structured in different ways.
Phonics & spelling	1	Word reading: To respond speedily to the correct sound to graphemes for all 40+ phonemes.
	2	Word reading: To read accurately by recognising the alternative sounds for graphemes.
	3	Transcription: To learn to spell common exception words.
	4	Word reading: To read words with contractions.
		Transcription: To learn to spell more words with contracted forms.
Plot, character & setting	1	Composition: To join clauses using 'and'. To learn how to use expanded noun phrases.
	2	Word reading: To learn how to use coordination (using 'but').
	3	Word reading: To read words containing common suffixes.
	4	Comprehension: To make inferences on the basis of what is being said and done.
	5	Comprehension: To discuss the sequence of events in books.
		Composition: To learn how to use the present and past tense correctly and consistently.
	6	Transcription: To learn to spell the days of the week.
		Comprehension: To discuss the sequence of events.
Talk about it	1	Spoken language: To give well-structured descriptions, explanations and narratives.
	2	Spoken language: To consider and evaluate different viewpoints.
	3	Comprehension: To recite some poems by heart.
	4	Spoken language: To participate in performances and role play.
	5	Spoken language: To use spoken language to develop understanding through exploring ideas.
	6	Spoken language: To ask relevant questions to extend understanding.
Get writing	1	Composition: To compose a sentence orally before writing it. To form short narratives.
	2	Composition: To develop positive attitudes and stamina by writing narratives.
	3	Composition: To write down ideas and key words.
		Composition: To develop positive attitudes and stamina for writing by writing poetry.
	4	Composition: To learn how to use subordination and coordination.
	5	Composition: To develop positive attitudes and stamina for writing by writing for different purposes. To proofread to check for errors.
	6	Composition: To develop positive attitudes by writing for different purposes.
Assessment	1	Comprehension: To explain clearly their understanding of what is read to them.
	2	Comprehension: To understand books by drawing on what they already know.
	3	Comprehension: To discuss and clarify the meanings of words.
	4	Comprehension: To understand books by asking and answering questions.

THE LIGHTHOUSE KEEPER'S LUNCH

About the book

First published in 1977, *The Lighthouse Keeper's Lunch* by Ronda and David Armitage has remained a bestseller ever since.

Every morning, come rain or shine, Mr Grinling travels out to his lighthouse. Every day, Mrs Grinling makes Mr Grinling a tasty picnic lunch and sends it across to him on a wire. One day, however, a group of seagulls discovers the flying lunch and eats the lot. Mrs Grinling tries different ways to stop the seagulls eating the picnic: she ties a napkin to the top and she sends the pet cat in the basket, but neither of these ideas work. In the end, she fills the sandwiches with mustard and the seagulls leave to find their lunch elsewhere.

The Lighthouse Keeper's Lunch has been a favourite class book for primary school teachers since its publication. It is engaging and clearly sequenced plot, distinct characters and attractive setting provide a wealth of activity opportunities – both for literacy and cross-curricular subjects.

Despite its short length, *The Lighthouse Keeper's Lunch* has a rich and varied vocabulary, with many glorious adjectives and adverbs. While Key Stage 1 children might need help reading and understanding these, once they know the words they can enjoy a level of poetic writing not usually found in picture books. The vocabulary will also lead to work on noun phrases, adjectives and adverbs. Similarly, the book will also support activities on learning the days of the week, writing recipes, poems and diaries.

For cross-curricular work, art and design projects to create seascapes and model lighthouses will make an attractive classroom display. Further cross-curricular work can be incorporated for geography (vocabulary for key features – cliff, sea, weather), history (how life has changed), science (identifying seagulls, the seasons) and design and technology (designing a system to deliver sandwiches to a lighthouse).

About the author

Ronda Armitage was born and grew up in New Zealand. She spent much of her childhood by the sea often playing around in boats and in the water. She moved to the UK in her early twenties. On the long boat journey to England, she met David Armitage. She has written nine books about the lighthouse keeper Mr Grinling as well as other titles, including three books about Small Knight and George. While writing books, Ronda Armitage has worked as a teacher, a care worker and a librarian.

About the illustrator

David Armitage was born in Tasmania and moved to the UK as a young man. He works as a fine artist.

Key facts

The Lighthouse Keeper's Lunch

Author: Ronda Armitage

Illustrator: David Armitage

First published: 1977 by Andre Deutsch Ltd

Awards: The Esther Glen Award for Best Book of the Year, New Zealand 1978

GUIDED READING

Introducing the book

Look together at the cover of *The Lighthouse Keeper's Lunch*. Ask the children to point out the lighthouse, the lighthouse keeper and the lunch. Ask: *What's happening to the basket? Where has it come from?* Listen to the children's ideas and suggest that you read the book to find out. Turn to the title page and ask the children to tell you what they see. Ask: *Has anyone seen seagulls at the seaside? What were they doing?* Ask the children to predict what might happen in the story.

First reading

Read *The Lighthouse Keeper's Lunch*. Don't worry too much about the difficult words – allow the story to carry them through. But do point out the detail in the illustrations as you read: the wire between the cottage and the lighthouse, the contrast between the rainy and sunny days, the light and dark as Mr Grinling lies in bed. Pause on the page with the food that Mrs Grinling has prepared. Ask: *Which food here would you most like to eat? Can you describe it? I'd like to eat the Peach Surprise because it looks so creamy and fruity.* Ask: *What do you usually have for lunch? Would you eat as much as Mr Grinling?* Agree that Mr Grinling's lunch is huge and sumptuous and more like a feast than a lunch. Carry on reading the story, putting on different voices for the seagulls and Mr Grinling, if possible.

Help the children to empathise with Mr Grinling's anger when the seagulls eat his lunch. Ask: *What can Mr and Mrs Grinling do to stop the birds eating the food? How would you feel if they ate your lunch?* Listen to the children's ideas, adding in ideas of your own (perhaps Mr Grinling could take the food with him in the boat, or Mrs Grinling could put a radio playing loud music in the basket).

Carry on reading, checking for understanding. Point out Mr Grinling's and Hamish's facial expressions and ask the children to infer how the characters are feeling. Ask: *What might Mr Grinling and Hamish say?* Check that the children know that mustard is very strong-tasting and can create a burning feeling in one's mouth.

Rich language

Now they know the story, read the book again, asking the children to join in. Help them to use their phonics to segment and blend words as you go along. Point out the long vowel sounds that you encounter and talk about any tricky words that they know and you want them to read without sounding out.

Pause to discuss the glorious (but difficult) vocabulary as you encounter each word, for example: 'perched', 'industrious', 'tended', 'concocting', 'appetising', 'devoured', 'gusto', 'varmints', 'scrumptious', 'baffle', 'racked their brains', 'brazen lot', 'accomplished', 'ingenious plan', 'secured', 'lackaday', 'expectant'. Ask older or more confident children to suggest what the words mean. Talk about why the author might have chosen that word rather than an easier word, for example why 'concocting' rather than 'making'? Ask the children if they like the words in the book. Ask them to discuss question 8 on the bookmark with a partner (page 10).

Focus on setting

Ask: *What is the setting for this book?* (The rocky coast.) Ask the children about times when they have been to the seaside. Is there anything from *The Lighthouse Keeper's Lunch* that reminds them of their trip to the sea? Have they seen cliffs and a lighthouse?

Explain the function of the lighthouse. Ask the children to discuss question 1 on the bookmark with their partner (looking after the light). Explain that the lighthouse works using lights and mirrors and that these must be cleaned daily so that the light shines brightly. Look at the picture of Mr Grinling in his bed and together discuss questions 5 and 9 on the bookmark, first explaining the meaning of 'tended'. Ask if the children would like to work in a lighthouse. As a group, discuss question 6 on the bookmark. Ask: *Do Mr and Mrs Grinling enjoy their work?* Discuss question 10.

Ask the children to find the two different places within this setting. Agree that there is the lighthouse (Mr Grinling's domain) and the cottage (Mrs Grinling's domain). Which setting would they like to be in? Look at the picture of Mr Grinling in the rain and carry out the description work in question 6 on the bookmark. Point out to the children that between the two settings is the sea, which is where the seagulls live and which the lunch has to pass safely through. Ask the children to work with a partner to look at each page in turn in the book and decide whether the location is the cottage or the lighthouse (or between the two).

Focus on plot

Challenge the children to find the days of the week, Monday to Saturday, in the book. Try to work out together what happens on each day. Together, look at each event in turn and ask the children, using the pictures and the story, to infer what the characters are thinking at each point. Discuss questions 2 and 3 on the bookmark. (Hamish does not want to get in the basket and feels sick; he's possibly scared of seagulls. The mustard sandwiches are too hot for the seagulls.) Ask the children to discuss question 7 with their partner, and then together agree what the speech bubbles tell us. Ask the children to read the words the seagulls say when they taste the mustard, using expressive voices. Look at the picture of the seagulls eating the fisherman's lunch and discuss the answer to questions 4 and 11 on the bookmark. Look at the last page and discuss how Mr Grinling feels.

Retelling and reflection

After reading, ask the children to tell their neighbour what they most liked about the story. As a group, share the different favourite elements, encouraging the children to elaborate on their thoughts. Write on the board the words 'On Monday…, On Tuesday…' and so on and ask the children to work in pairs to retell the story together. Finally, ask the pairs to discuss question 12 on the bookmark.

■SCHOLASTIC
READ & RESPOND
Bringing the best books to life in the classroom

■SCHOLASTIC
READ & RESPOND
Bringing the best books to life in the classroom

The Lighthouse Keeper's Lunch by Ronda and David Armitage

The Lighthouse Keeper's Lunch by Ronda and David Armitage

Focus on...
Meaning

1. What is the main job that Mr Grinling has to do at the lighthouse?

2. Why is Hamish unable to scare the seagulls?

3. Why do the seagulls not want to eat the mustard sandwiches?

4. If you were the fisherman at the end, how would you scare away the seagulls?

Focus on...
Organisation

5. Look at the picture of Mr Grinling in bed. Why is he smiling?

6. Look at the picture of Mr Grinling in the rain. Describe the weather to your partner.

7. What do the words in the speech bubbles tell us?

Focus on...
Language and features

8. Would you rather eat a 'sumptuous' meal or a 'nice' meal?

9. What does the caring word 'tended' tell us about how Mr Grinling feels about the lighthouse?

Focus on...
Purpose, viewpoints and effects

10. How would you describe Mrs Grinling?

11. Do you think the seagulls were naughty to eat the lunch?

12. What could happen in another story about the Grinlings?

Extract 1

- Display and read together Extract 1. Ask: *What part of the book is this?* Circle the words 'There once was' and talk about other ways that stories open. ('Once upon a time', 'A long time ago', 'One day', 'Jack woke up' and so on).

- Explain that story openings often quickly introduce the main character and the setting. Ask a volunteer to circle these in the extract (Mr Grinling, the cottage, the lighthouse).

- Underline the long /igh/ phoneme in 'lighthouse' and model reading the word. Together, list the other ways that this phoneme can be spelled ('i–e' and 'y'). Challenge the children to find and underline six more words with the /igh/ phoneme ('night', 'white', 'time', 'high', 'shine' and 'light'). Talk about the pronunciation of 'lived' with a short /i/ phoneme.

- Highlight the word 'perched'. Ask: *What does this word tell us that 'sat' doesn't?* Help the children to read and understand the words *industrious* and *tended*, bringing out the positive nature of these words. Ask: *What do we learn about Mr Grinling from this extract?* (That he works hard whatever the weather and that he looks after his light in a caring way.)

Extract 2

- Display an enlarged version of Extract 2. Circle 'appear', 'accomplished', 'ingenious', 'guard', 'secured', 'consolingly' and 'herring'. Demonstrate using phonics to read 'accomplished'. Ask pairs to read the other circled words and discuss a possible meaning. Share the correct pronunciations and meanings.

- Ask: *What is the extract about?* (Using Hamish to frighten the seagulls.) *What are Mr and Mrs Grinling going to get Hamish to do?* (Go in a basket next to the food.) Ask the children to infer how Hamish feels about the plan. (Very bad, scared, angry.) Ask: *How do you know this?* (He spits and hisses; he is rigid in the illustration.) Ask the children in pairs to role play an unhappy Hamish and a consoling Mrs Grinling.

- Ask one side of the room to argue in favour of the plan (seagulls are frightened of cats; Hamish might be able to hiss at the seagulls; the seagulls will be shocked when they see the lunch move; Hamish will be pleased to have some herring). Ask the other side to argue against the plan (Hamish doesn't like seagulls; Hamish doesn't want to go in the basket; Hamish might fall out of the basket; Hamish might feel sick; the seagulls might attack Hamish).

Extract 3

- Display an enlarged version of Extract 3. Ask: *What sort of text is this?* (Information text.) Recap on 'fiction' and 'non-fiction' and agree that this extract is non-fiction and that *The Lighthouse Keeper's Lunch* is fiction.

- Ask the children to point out the non-fiction features in this extract. Together, locate the subheadings, the caption and the label.

- Read the extract together and explain that glass of different shapes makes a beam of light change direction. Ask: *How does the illustration help you to understand how a lighthouse works?*

- Point out the use of straightforward non-fiction words: 'tall building', 'strong light', 'dangerous rocks', 'shaped glass'. Next, point out the words that are special to the subject: 'beam' and 'prism'.

Extract 1

Once there was a lighthouse keeper called Mr Grinling. At night time he lived in a small white cottage perched high on the cliffs. In the day time he rowed out to his lighthouse on the rocks to clean and polish the light.

Mr Grinling was a most industrious lighthouse keeper. Come rain...

   ...or shine, he tended his light.

Extract 2

"Our cat does not appear to like seagulls," said Mrs Grinling.

"No, my dear," said Mr Grinling, "Hamish is an accomplished seagull chaser."

"Of course," exclaimed Mrs Grinling, "tomorrow Hamish can guard the lunch."

"A most ingenious plan," agreed Mr Grinling.

Hamish did not think that this plan was ingenious at all. He spat and hissed as Mrs Grinling secured him in the basket.

"There, there, Hamish," said Mrs Grinling consolingly, "I'll have a tasty piece of herring waiting for you when you arrive home."

Extract 3

How a lighthouse works

A lighthouse is a tall building that shines out a strong light to warn ships about dangerous rocks.

The rocks near this lighthouse are dangerous to ships.

Inside a lighthouse

A lighthouse has many stairs to take the keeper up to the light at the top.

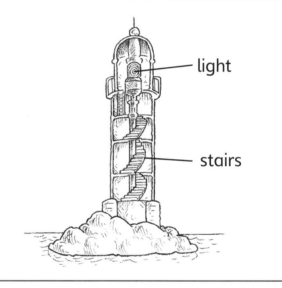

light

stairs

Inside the light

Shaped glass (called prisms) around the light point the light into a beam.

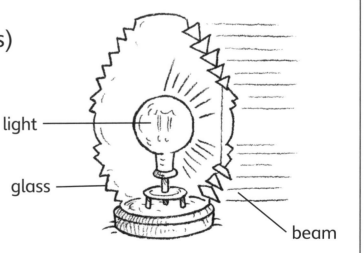

light

glass

beam

PHONICS & SPELLING

1. Long vowel scavenge

Objective
To know the different graphemes for the long vowel phonemes.

What you need
Copies of *The Lighthouse Keeper's Lunch*, printable page 'Long vowel scavenge', interactive activity 'Long vowel baskets'.

What to do
- Recap on the main spelling options for the long vowel phonemes. Remind the children that while 'ea' is the /ee/ phoneme, 'ear' is the /ear/ phoneme.

- Provide the children with printable page 'Long vowel scavenge'. Ask them to find a word for each slot on the page. Tell them to colour in a layer of the lighthouse each time they fill in a word. Can they reach the top?

- Write the words 'give' and 'glove' on the board. Remind the children that these are exception words with short /i/ and /u/ phonemes. Ask the children to complete the challenge at the bottom of the page and colour in the light.

Differentiation
Support: Carry out interactive activity 'Long vowel baskets'. Tell the children to drag and drop words into the lunch basket with the correct long vowel phoneme. Explain that first they have two baskets to choose from, then three, then four.

Extension: Challenge children to find two words in the story where the long /oa/ phoneme is spelled with 'o' ('most', 'gusto'). Ask them to learn to spell the following words: 'white', 'lived', 'lighthouse', 'keeper', 'sea', 'tomorrow', 'most'.

2. Sound sort

Objective
To know the alternative sounds for graphemes.

What you need
Copies of *The Lighthouse Keeper's Lunch*, printable page 'Sound sort', scissors.

What to do
- Write the words 'hive', 'top', 'farm' and 'hint' on the board. Ask volunteers to come to the front and read the words and underline the grapheme making the vowel phoneme.

- Remind the children that although these words follow the normal rules for English, there are many words that we need to learn that have alternative pronunciations.

- Write the words 'lived', 'most', 'warm', 'gusto', 'have' and 'mind'. (Find them together in *The Lighthouse Keeper's Lunch* if time allows.)

- Help the children to read these words and underline the graphemes for them. Ask them to tell you how the pronunciation of these vowel graphemes differs from how they would normally expect to pronounce them.

- Provide pairs with printable page 'Sound sort'. Ask them to cut out the words from the page and sort them into piles on top of each phoneme.

Differentiation
Support: Provide the children with only the first two rows of words to sort.
Extension: Challenge more confident learners, in pairs, to read another picture book together and draw up a list of words they find that have non-standard pronunciations. (Remind them that many will be high-frequency words.)

3. Lighthouse bingo

Objective

To read common exception words.

What you need

Enlarged version of printable page 'Lighthouse bingo' cut up into six bingo cards, all the words from the cards on separate slips in a hat.

What to do

- Work with a group of 12 children, asking the children to work in pairs. Give each pair a bingo card.

- Ask the pairs to read the words on their card, discussing the parts of the words that make the word tricky to read or spell.

- Pull the words from the hat one by one. Tell the children to cross out the words on their card as they hear you read them out.

- Tell the children to shout out 'line' if they complete a line of crossed off words, and 'house' if they cross out all the words on their bingo card.

- Remind the children who don't win that this is just a game of luck (plus listening).

Differentiation

Support: Create easier bingo grids using the words you would like your children to learn.
Extension: Challenge more confident learners to make new bingo grids using words you want them to learn, or the trickier words from the book.

4. A good ending

Objective

To read and spell words with contractions.

What you need

Copies of *The Lighthouse Keeper's Lunch*, printable page 'She's great'.

What to do

- Read the words spoken by the seagulls in *The Lighthouse Keeper's Lunch*. In each instance (apart from the page where they eat the mustard), write down the word with a contraction ('she's', 'they'll', 'aren't', 'let's', 'it's' and 'we'll'). Ask the children to tell you the long form of the word each time and re-read the sentence using the longer version (for example, 'She is a great cook, Fred.')

- Provide further examples to read and write out in full as a group: 'he's fine', 'the cat's asleep', 'he'll go', 'she'll stay', 'don't cry', 'it won't move' and so on.

- Hand out copies of printable page 'She's great' (choosing to give just the top half for Year 1 children if appropriate) and ask the children to complete the activity.

Differentiation

Support: Use the words on the top half of the printable page to create an activity page where less confident learners draw a line from the contraction to the longer version.
Extension: Ask more confident children to provide you with contractions for: 'they are', 'we are', 'the boys will', 'Sam will', 'the day is long' and 'the sea will wash it away'.

PLOT, CHARACTER & SETTING

1. Lighthouse setting

Objectives

To combine ideas in sentences with 'and'.
To write expanded noun phrases.

What you need

Media resources 'Lighthouses' and 'Seaside sounds', interactive activity 'Lighthouse labelling', individual whiteboards and pens, craft materials, slips of paper.

What to do

- Display and discuss the media resource 'Lighthouses' (three photographs of different lighthouses), then listen to media resource 'Seaside sounds'. Capture a range of nouns and adjectives, asking children to write words on their individual whiteboards first each time.

- Model using the words to write expanded noun phrases on the board (tall lighthouse, shining light, dangerous rocks and so on).

- Ask the children to carry out interactive activity 'Lighthouse labelling'.

- Provide a range of card and paints and ask the children to plan how they could make a lighthouse model. Discuss and modify ideas before making a classroom display. Create rocks out of papier-mâché or clay. Scrunch up coloured paper or cellophane to make waves. Paint a seascape backdrop, perhaps showing stormy and clear on different parts of the image.

- Ask the children to write a caption for part of the model: a simple sentence with a capital letter and a full stop (The lighthouse is tall.), a sentence using the word 'and' (The sea is rough and scary. The wind is noisy and the sea is wild.), or an expanded noun phrase (tall, white lighthouse, dangerous rocks).

Differentiation

Support: Provide sentence starters to complete, or adjectives and nouns to combine.

2. Opposites

Objective

To join clauses with 'but'.

What you need

Copies of *The Lighthouse Keeper's Lunch*, interactive activity 'Light and dark', individual whiteboards and pens, lamp.

Cross-curricular link

Geography

What to do

- Look together at the spread in the book showing Mr Grinling in bed. Point out that there are lots of opposites in this picture: the warm bed/the cold sea, the dark night/the bright light, Mr Grinling at rest/the sailors on the boat working.

- Provide the children with interactive activity 'Light and dark' and ask them to find the opposites of the words or phrases shown.

- Write the following sentence on the board: The night is dark but the light is bright.

- Challenge the children, in pairs, to create a sentence together for the lighthouse and cottage that uses 'but' (for example 'The lighthouse is tall but the cottage is little.', 'Mr Grinling works in the lighthouse but sleeps in the cottage.'). Let them attempt to write their sentence on their individual whiteboard and hold it up. Repeat with three more sentences.

- Add a lamp underneath the lighthouse in your display and see how well it shines with the classroom curtains closed.

Differentiation

Support: Provide sentence starters such as: 'The lighthouse is at sea but the cottage…' or 'Sometimes the sea is stormy but…' or even complete sentences cut in half which the children match up.
Extension: Ask early finishers to write a descriptive sentence for the page where Mr Grinling is in bed.

3. Meet Mr and Mrs Grinling

Objective

To read and write words with suffixes ('ly' and 'ful').

What you need

Photocopiable page 20 'Adding 'ly' and 'ful'', copies of *The Lighthouse Keeper's Lunch*.

What to do

- Write 'Mr Grinling' and 'Mrs Grinling' as headings on the board. Divide the class and ask one half to write words (with an adult scribe) about Mr Grinling and the other about Mrs Grinling – these can be nouns, adjectives or phrases (hard working, clever, stays in the house, works at the lighthouse and so on). Swap after a few minutes.

- Make models of Mr and Mrs Grinling for your display and add the best words from the list.

- Remind the children of the tricky words 'industrious' and 'consolingly' and find them in the story. Ask the children to role play Mr Grinling being industrious and Mrs Grinling consoling Hamish.

- Write the word 'consolingly' on the board and demonstrate how it comprises a root ('consoling') and a suffix ('ly'). Ask for other words ending in 'ly' (badly, quietly, happily, kindly and so on) and ask the children to help you split each word into root and suffix (providing more support for words such as 'happily', which need to change).

- Distribute photocopiable page 20 'Adding 'ly' and 'ful'' and ask the children to complete the task.

Differentiation

Support: Ask less confident learners to focus on the first half of the activity. Provide the root and suffixes as cards for the children to experiment putting together and reading the new word.
Extension: Ask more confident learners to add 'ly' to 'happy', 'tidy' and 'snappy', and 'ful' to 'beauty'.

4. What a brazen lot

Objective

To make inferences on the basis of what is being said and done.

What you need

Media resource 'Seagull sounds', copies of *The Lighthouse Keeper's Lunch*.

Cross-curricular link

Science

What to do

- Display media resource 'Seagull sounds' and listen to the seagulls. Ask pairs to talk about the sounds the seagulls make and then share these as a class. (Noisy, mocking, laughing, calling to each other and so on.)

- Provide groups of three with a copy of *The Lighthouse Keeper's Lunch*. Ask them to read the seagull conversations together, each taking one of the speech bubbles and putting on different voices if possible. Afterwards, ask them to discuss what sort of characters the seagulls are. Are they hard-working like Mr Grinling? Are they clever like Mrs Grinling?

- Ask each trio to create some comments for the seagulls after they've recovered from eating the mustard. What might they say to each other?

- Ask each group to draw a seagull, write a speech bubble for it and add it to the display.

- Now ask them to look at Hamish in his flying basket. Ask them to discuss what he might say to his best friend about his trip. Can they infer what Hamish thinks about seagulls and his trip?

Differentiation

Support: Ask less confident learners to pretend to be naughty seagulls stealing Mr Grinling's food. Can they show through acting what sort of characters the seagulls are?
Extension: Ask early finishers to create speech bubbles for the three seagulls on the title page.

5. In the right order

Objectives

To discuss the sequence of events in books.
To use the past tense consistently.

What you need

Photocopiable page 21 'Sort it out', an A5 booklet for each child made by folding two A4 sheets in half and stapling along the spine.

What to do

- As a class, remember the plot of *The Lighthouse Keeper's Lunch*. Remind the children that the story takes place in the past. Model saying sentences in the past tense.

- Provide each child with photocopiable page 21 'Sort it out' and an A5 booklet. Ask them to cut out the images from the photocopiable sheet and stick them in order into their booklet – one image per page, leaving the first page blank to be the cover.

- Tell the children to turn to their partner and tell them the story, saying a sentence for each picture. Remind the children to help each other to use the past tense for their sentences.

- Ask the children to write a sentence underneath each picture and to create a front cover for their book.

- Tell the children to check their story and then swap with another child. They should check for capital letters, full stops and past tense.

Differentiation

Support: Carry out this activity as a piece of shared writing, scribing for the children.
Extension: Challenge more confident learners to write elegant sentences and to read their work to the class.

6. On Monday...

Objectives

To spell the days of the week.
To discuss the sequence of events in books.

What you need

Copies of *The Lighthouse Keeper's Lunch*, printable page 'On Monday...', scissors.

What to do

- Ask the children to work with a partner to find the days of the week in *The Lighthouse Keeper's Lunch* and to work out what happened on each day.

- Provide each pair with a copy of printable page 'On Monday...' and ask them to cut out the events and to stick them against the correct day.

- Once the pages have dried, ask the children to colour in each event using the following code:
  - Yellow: everything is happy for the Grinlings.
  - Orange: things start to go wrong.
  - Red: things continue to go wrong.
  - Purple: things begin to go right.

- When the children have finished, discuss the path of the story, writing the events on the board using the shape of a story mountain (with the red events at the top). Explain that many stories have this pattern. Ask: *What do you think the Grinlings do on a Sunday?*

- Practise spelling the days of the week, taking particular care over 'Wednesday'.

Differentiation

Support: Provide less confident learners with a completed copy of printable page 'On Monday...' and ask them to tick off the events as they find them in the book.
Extension: Provide more confident learners with the printable sheet without the prompts at the bottom to cut out. Ask them to make notes for the events against each day.

Adding 'ly' and 'ful'

- Read these words from *The Lighthouse Keeper's Lunch*.
- Split the words up into their two parts: root and ending.
- Write the two parts.

brightly   _____   _____

clearly   _____   _____

sadly   _____   _____

thoughtful   _____   _____

- Add 'ly' or 'ful' to each word to create a new one.

pain_____

bad_____

slow_____

joy_____

poor_____

cheer_____

kind_____

help_____

Sort it out

- Cut out these images from *The Lighthouse Keepers Lunch*.
- Stick them in an eight-page booklet in the right order, starting on page 2.
- Write a sentence underneath each picture. Give your book a front and back cover.

TALK ABOUT IT

1. News flash

Objective

To give well-structured descriptions, explanations and narratives.

What you need

Media resource 'Cliff scene', printable page 'News flash', simple recording devices, fake microphone, dressing-up clothes.

Cross-curricular link

Computing

What to do

- Ask the children if they've ever seen a news report. Explain the format using the structure from printable page 'News flash'.

- Organise the children into groups of six and give each group the printable sheet. Ask them to use the ideas to plan their report and decide who will take on each role. Make costumes available.

- Allow time for the children to plan and then practise creating their report. Remind them to speak clearly and that a few interesting words is all they need to say.

- Create an area with a desk for the news anchor (making a sign if possible) and another area with media resource 'Cliff scene' displayed. This will be the backdrop for the interview with Mr and Mrs Grinling.

- Organise the groups to come to the front and help them to record their news report, pausing the film between scenes.

- Share and enjoy the news clips the children have created.

Differentiation

Support: Provide less confident learners with scripted answers with which to take on the role of Mr or Mrs Grinling.
Extension: Encourage more confident and organised learners to lead the group.

2. Seagull solutions

Objective

To consider and evaluate different viewpoints.

What you need

Printable page 'Seagull solutions'.

Cross-curricular link

Design & technology

What to do

- Ask the children: *How did Mrs Grinling defeat the seagulls?* (She made mustard sandwiches.) *Can you think of another way to defeat the seagulls?* Collect all the ideas on the board (with the exception of any violent ideas that end with seagull deaths) and ask the children to articulate further how they think these ideas might work.

- Organise the children into groups and give each group printable page 'Seagull solutions'. Read the page with the class and then ask each group to talk about the merits of each idea. Rank the ideas from 1 to 5, explaining that everyone in the group must agree to the ranking and must have a chance to speak and be listened to.

- Ask each group draw a picture of the favourite seagull solution and talk about how it might work. Ask each group to present their idea to the class. (Allow them to be rather fantastical about their solutions.)

Differentiation

Extension: Ask more confident learners to draw a series of images showing how the seagull solution works. Encourage them to use more of their own ideas.

3. Recite a poem

Objective
To recite some poems by heart.

What you need
Photocopiable page 25 'The Picnic', recording equipment.

Cross-curricular links
Computing, science

What to do
- Together, read an enlarged copy of photocopiable page 25 'The Picnic'. Point out the rhyming words (box/Socks, fun/one) and their spellings. Discuss the use of capital letters for 'Hats', 'Shoes' and 'Socks'.

- Organise the children into groups to create a performance of the poem, learning some of the poem by heart if possible. Explain that they can recite the poem together, or half of them can take each verse, or they can take a line or a sentence each.

- Ask children to draw images to use as props, perhaps drawing a cross over the hats, shoes and socks. Other children might like to create a slideshow of seaside images and recite their poem as this is being displayed. Point out the important elements of performance: stance, voice, expression and so on.

- Record the groups' performances. If different children are reading different lines, press pause between lines as they organise themselves so that you are able to get a close-up of each child in the same position. Hopefully the poem will flow seamlessly when you play the video.

Differentiation
Support: Encourage less confident learners to learn a line in pairs. Provide them with simple recording devices such as 'talking tins' to help them.

Extension: Encourage more confident learners to think creatively about how they could record their poem using video and still photographs to create a fun video.

4. Act it out

Objective
To participate in performances and role play.

What you need
Printable page 'The Lighthouse Keeper's playscript'.

Cross-curricular link
Design & technology

What to do
- Display an enlarged version of printable page 'The Lighthouse Keeper's Playscript'. Explain the features of a playscript. Allocate a part from the script to different tables in the room. Read the text a few times, asking the tables of children to say their lines.

- In a large space, reorganise the children into groups containing one person from each table and ask the groups to act out the scene. Allow the children to either read the lines or improvise their own version.

- Ask the children to continue the story and improvise Mrs Grinling making mustard sandwiches and the seagulls eating them.

- As a class, design, create, test and improve a system to send a basket across the room and use this in the performances. Remind the children that the actors playing the seagulls will need to be able to reach the basket.

- Share the different scenes with the rest of the class.

Differentiation
Support: Ask less confident learners to take on the role of extra seagulls. Some of these children might prefer to work backstage and operate the basket.

Extension: Ask more confident learners to create a dramatic version of the whole book.

TALK ABOUT IT

5. Food, glorious food

Objective
To use spoken language to explore ideas.

What you need
Copies of *The Lighthouse Keeper's Lunch*, a range of foods to try.

What to do
- Discuss the children's favourite foods, creating a list of adjectives used for food and a list of foods discussed.

- Try the foods that you have brought in (being aware of any children with food allergies) and together choose a range of adjectives to describe each food.

- Organise the children into groups and ask them to look at the spread of food prepared by Mrs Grinling in *The Lighthouse Keeper's Lunch*. Tell them to talk about each dish in turn and to speculate about what it comprises, how it tastes, what its texture might be and whether they would enjoy eating it. Suggest that they look at the list of adjectives drawn up earlier to help them describe foods. Remind them to listen to each other's opinion and comment on what their group members say. Ask them to discuss which part of the lunch would be their favourite.

- Pause halfway through the conversation and quiz children about what their group members have said.

- Afterwards discuss each food in turn, pointing out that we can only speculate about the contents of the seafood salad and the sandwich. Scribe for the class as they create a sentence about each item.

- Carry out a class survey to find out which is their favourite food from *The Lighthouse Keeper's Lunch*.

Differentiation
Support: Provide a range of ingredients and adjectives written on slips of paper for less confident learners to place against the foods on the page.
Extension: Require more confident learners to create an oral sentence about each food.

6. Question time

Objective
To ask relevant questions.

What you need
Costume as Mr or Mrs Grinling (optional), printable page 'Question time'.

What to do
- Come into the room in character as Mr or Mrs Grinling, with some sort of costume or prop if possible. Sit on the 'hot-seat' and ask the children if they have any questions for either Mr or Mrs Grinling and answer their questions.

- Explain to the children that volunteers can take the hot-seat as Mr Grinling, Mrs Grinling, Bert the seagull and Hamish the cat and the class needs to prepare some questions to ask the characters. In pairs, ask the children to complete the printable page 'Question time'. This page will help them to generate four questions to ask the characters in the story.

- Ask volunteers or different children to take the 'hot-seat' in role as Mr Grinling, Mrs Grinling, a seagull and Hamish. Encourage the children to ask the questions they have generated on their printable page and any other questions. Help the children to think of further lines of questioning.

Differentiation
Support: Provide completed questions for less confident learners to choose from and ask clearly.
Extension: Challenge more confident learners to ask unique questions when the questions are drying up in the hot-seating session.

The Picnic

We brought a rug for sitting on,

Our lunch was in a box.

The sand was warm. We didn't wear

Hats or Shoes or Socks.

Waves came curling up the beach.

We waded. It was fun.

Our sandwiches were different kinds.

I dropped my jelly one.

Dorothy Aldis

GET WRITING

1. Mrs Grinling's diary

Objective

To write a narrative.

What you need

Diary entries for your own week, simple but using details that the children will recognise.

What to do

- Display your diary entries for the week so far, for example: 'Today we started reading *The Lighthouse Keeper's Lunch* in class. I was pleased that the children enjoyed it. I had cottage pie for lunch. It was delicious.'

- Talk about the features of the text: capital letters, full stops, written in the past tense. Point out that the entry says what happened and how you felt about it.

- Ask pairs to recap on Mrs Grinling's week.

- Write the days of the week on the board and fill in notes about Mrs Grinling's week, capturing key vocabulary.

- Ask the children to write a diary for the week for Mrs Grinling, writing at least one sentence for each day (with a capital letter and a full stop), orally rehearsing each sentence first and checking afterwards. Can they write how Mrs Grinling felt on at least two days? Model using 'and' or 'but' to extend a sentence: 'I made a lovely lunch for Mr Grinling but it didn't get to him.' 'I put Hamish in the basket and put the basket on the wire.'

- Use peer review to share and improve their writing.

Differentiation

Support: Groups of six can talk about each entry and then write one entry each.

Extension: More confident learners could include different types of sentence in their writing, such as exclamations and questions. They could also practise using 'if', 'when', 'because' and time/ordering connectives.

2. The Lighthouse Keeper's Bad Day

Objective

To write a narrative.

What you need

Photocopiable page 29 'Mr Grinling's Bad Day'.

What to do

- Tell the children that they are going to be writing a new adventure for the lighthouse keeper. Draw a 'story mountain' on the board and talk about how things get worse (top of the mountain) then better (bottom of the mountain) for the Grinlings in *The Lighthouse Keeper's Lunch*. Tell the children that they are going to use this structure for their new story.

- Discuss ideas for this new story, for example: the light goes out in the lighthouse; a hole in the boat strands Mr Grinling on shore or at the lighthouse; Mr Grinling breaks his leg and Mrs Grinling has to go and clean the light; the seagulls come back; Mr Grinling goes on holiday and the new lighthouse keeper is very bad.

- Distribute photocopiable page 29 'Mr Grinling's Bad Day'. Provide versions enlarged onto A3 paper if necessary. Tell the children to use it to plan the story on the chart, and then storyboard their story and tell it to three different people.

- Tell the children to give feedback on the stories and use it they receive to improve their story (redrawing pictures or changing their oral story in their heads).

- Tell the children to write a sentence for each picture to tell their story.

Differentiation

Support: Ask less confident learners to write labels for their picture, or to just focus on telling their oral story.

Extension: Encourage more confident learners to use adjectives and adverbs in their story.

3. At the seaside

Objectives

To write poetry.
To write down ideas including key words.

What you need

Media resources 'Lighthouses', 'Waves are fun' and 'Seaside sounds'.

What to do

- Explain to the children that they will be writing a poem about the sea. Look together at photographs 1 and 3 from media resource 'Lighthouses', then at media resource 'Waves are fun' and then the sounds of the storm in media resource 'Seaside sounds'. Use these to create a long class list of seaside vocabulary, putting nouns and adjectives on different sides of the board: 'choppy', 'spray', 'blue', 'grey', 'sparkly', 'stormy', 'hot', 'sticky', 'lazy', 'lighthouse', 'waves', 'ice cream', 'sand' and so on.

- Match nouns and adjectives: 'crashing waves', 'jumping children', 'sticky ice cream', 'hot sand'.

- Ask the children to create as many of their own seaside noun phrases as they can. Share lists in groups.

- Ask the children to choose their favourite six noun phrases and use them to write a list poem about the sea.

- Tell the children to swap their poem with a partner. Within their pairs, each child should share their favourite line from their partner's poem and one thing (spelling, word choice, order) that they might change about it.

- Let the children make final changes to their rough draft, taking on board their partner's comments, before writing out a final copy.

Differentiation

Support: Provide a range of words on slips of paper for less confident children to try out and stick down.
Extension: Expect interesting vocabulary and a polished order.

4. A postcard home

Objectives

To write narratives about personal experiences.
To use subordination and co-ordination.

What you need

Blank postcards, the children's own addresses, media resource 'Picture postcards', other written postcards, stamps (if budget allows).

What to do

- Look at and read media resource 'Picture postcards' and any postcards brought in.

- Ask: *Has anyone ever been to the seaside?* Share memories. Tell the children that they are going to write a holiday postcard from an imaginary trip to the seaside.

- Talk about the different things that happen on a seaside holiday and capture these as past tense phrases: *a seagull ate our lunch, we splashed in the waves, my sister dropped her ice cream.* Talk about the past tense and the suffix 'ed'.

- Hand out the blank postcards and help the children to fill in the name of someone in their household and their address. Model a format for the card: 'Dear…, We are at the seaside. Yesterday we…'. Ask them to write two sentences in the past tense, trying to use 'and', 'but' or 'because' at least once. ('We built a sandcastle but the sea washed it away.' 'I had an ice cream but I dropped it.')

- Remind the children to orally rehearse first, then write using phonic knowledge and check after.

- Stamp the postcards and walk to the post box together to post them.

Differentiation

Support: Help children to create one clear sentence using 'and', which you can scribe for them.
Extension: Challenge more confident learners to use 'when' or 'if' in one of their sentences.

5. How to make a Lighthouse Sandwich

Objectives

To write for different purposes.
To proofread to check for errors.

What you need

A range of sandwich fillings or coloured paper to represent them, interactive activity 'How to make a Lighthouse Sandwich', simple recipe books, copies of *The Lighthouse Keeper's Lunch.*

What to do

- Look at the image of the Lighthouse Sandwich in *The Lighthouse Keeper's Lunch*. Ask: *What might be in it?* Accept all reasonable suggestions and write them on the board.

- Recap on the features of instruction texts using a range of simple recipe books. Capture useful vocabulary on the board: 'What you need, What to do, First, Carefully, Next' and so on.

- Ask the children to work with a partner to orally rehearse a recipe for the Lighthouse Sandwich, explaining that they can decide what goes in it – but remind them that it needs something red, something green and something yellow (and it should sound tasty as we know Mrs Grinling is a good cook).

- Ask the children to write out their recipe and then proofread it before passing it to a partner to check.

- Ask the children to take the real, or paper, ingredients and make their sandwich. Ask: *Were your recipes easy to follow? Did you miss anything out? Were your sandwiches tasty?*

Differentiation

Support: Ask less confident learners to carry out interactive activity 'How to make a Lighthouse Sandwich'.
Extension: Challenge more confident learners to use time words such as 'first', 'next' and 'then' in their recipe.

6. How the lunch reaches the lighthouse

Objective

To write for different purposes.

What you need

Photocopiable page 30 'How the lunch reaches the lighthouse', a rope and a basket, example explanation texts.

Cross-curricular link

Design & technology

What to do

- Ask: *How does Mr Grinling get the basket back to Mrs Grinling?* (Mr Grinling has to bring it back in the boat because the basket cannot travel up-hill.)

- Set up a rope across the classroom, with one end higher than the other, and then send a small basket down the rope. Allow the children to take turns. (Practise before the session to get the angle and tautness of the rope right so that the basket slides – but not too much.)

- Share some example explanation texts and ask the children to look at the diagrams, explanation sentences and labels. Ensure the information is at the correct reading level.

- Hand out individual copies of photocopiable page 30 'How the lunch reaches the lighthouse', and ask them to write an explanation text for this. Tell them to talk to their partner first about what might go in each label box, for example: 'The basket is put on the wire.' 'The basket travels down the wire.' 'The basket is taken off the wire.' Talk about what might be written at the bottom to explain the diagram, for example: 'The basket travels down the wire because the cottage is higher than the lighthouse.'

Differentiation

Support: Provide labels to stick in the correct place.
Extension: Expect a comprehensive sentence at the bottom of the page.

Mr Grinling's Bad Day

- Plan your story on the back of the sheet.
- Draw pictures to tell your story.

1. Beginning We meet Mr and Mrs Grinling.	**2. Things begin to go wrong.**
3. Things are still going wrong.	**4. The Grinlings' first idea doesn't make things better.**
5. A new idea works.	**6. The Grinlings are happy.**

How the lunch reaches the lighthouse

● Add labels and a caption to this diagram.

1. Mr Grinling's day

Objectives

To explain an understanding of the story.
To discuss the sequence of events in books.

What you need

Interactive activity 'Mr Grinling's day'.

What to do

- Ask the children to speculate in pairs about what Mrs Grinling's day might comprise. Share ideas, reminding the children that we don't know. Perhaps Mr Grinling brings her a cup of tea in bed before she gets up. What does she do in the afternoon? Perhaps she shops and plans the food for the next day, visits friends, writes a novel, goes to work, digs the garden and so on.

- Ask the children to carry out interactive activity 'Mr Grinling's day' independently. This activity asks the children to order a number of objects to capture Mr Grinling's morning routine. They then write some words to briefly describe what Mr Grinling does at each stage. The activity will mark the correct order of the images. Notes for each image should be along the lines of:
  - 'Mr Grinling gets up', 'gets up' or 'gets out of bed'.
  - 'Mr Grinling goes down the path to his boat', 'goes to boat' or 'boat'.
  - 'Mr Grinling rows out to the lighthouse', 'boat to lighthouse' or 'goes to lighthouse'.
  - 'Mr Grinling climbs the stairs to the light', 'climbs stairs' or 'goes up stairs'.
  - 'Mr Grinling cleans the lamp' or 'cleans light'.

Differentiation

Support: Encourage less confident learners to attempt to write a word or two. Ask them to describe to you orally what Mr Grinling does.
Extension: Require more confident learners to write a full sentence with a full stop for each picture.

2. What are they like?

Objectives

To explain an understanding of the story.
To draw on what they already know.

What you need

Interactive activity 'What are they like?'.

What to do

- Ask the children to carry out interactive activity 'What are they like?', explaining the activity to them. The activity will provide a score.

- After the interactive activity, complete the following on paper to be marked. Ask the children to remember the phrases used in the interactive activity. Ask them to combine two phrases with 'and' or 'but' to create a longer descriptive sentences. For example:
  - *Mr Grinling is hard working and likes to eat a big lunch.*
  - *Mr Grinling is hard working but he gets cross.*
  - *Mrs Grinling is clever and a good cook.*
  - *Mrs Grinling is good at having ideas and cooking.*

Differentiation

Support: Read all the words in the interactive activity to the children, ensuring that they understand the meaning of each before leaving them to carry out the activity independently.
Extension: Provide more confident learners with pictures of Mr and Mrs Grinling and ask them to write words about them around the picture. Ask early finishers to draw a picture of the seagulls and to write two words to describe them.

3. Delicious vocabulary

Objective

To discuss and clarify the meanings of words.

What you need

Interactive activity 'Delicious vocabulary'.

What to do

- Ask the children to carry out interactive activity 'Delicious vocabulary'. This activity will assess the children's understanding of the vocabulary in the story, first by asking them to match the word to its meaning, and then by choosing the correct word to complete a number of sentences.

- After the children have finished the activity, discuss the answers with them. As a class carry out an activity to create new sentences for the words.

- Ask: *Have you enjoyed learning these new words or do you prefer simple words? Why do authors sometimes use hard words?* (To get just the right meaning, for the love of language, for the poetic sound.)

- Ask: *Which is your favourite new word from the story?* Discuss the children's preferences, adding your own.

Differentiation

Support: Provide less confident learners with a version of the activity for the words you would like to assess them on.

Extension: Ask more confident learners to attempt to use the words from the activity in their own sentences. Allocate words as appropriate to the child.

4. True or false

Objective

To explain clearly an understanding of the story. To answer questions about books they have read.

What you need

Interactive activity 'True or false', individual whiteboards and pens.

What to do

- Make the following statement about *The Lighthouse Keeper's Lunch*: Mr Grinling works as a train driver. Agree that this statement is false.

- Make further statements and ask the children to write on their whiteboards 'True' or 'False' and hold them up. For example: Hamish is Mrs Grinling's pet parrot. Mrs Grinling makes Mr Grinling Peach Surprise for lunch. Mr Grinling listens to the boats hooting at night.

- Ask the children to carry out interactive activity 'True or false'.

Differentiation

Support: Allow less confident learners to carry out the assessment in pairs so they can discuss the answer together. Provide them with a copy of the book to use as they carry out the test.

Extension: Create your own more difficult quiz but using the statements on the interactive activity, plus these statements interspersed: The parrot is called Molly. The fisherman is Mr Grinling's brother. Mrs Grinling goes shopping in the afternoon. For each statement give these children the option of 'True', 'False' and 'We don't know'.